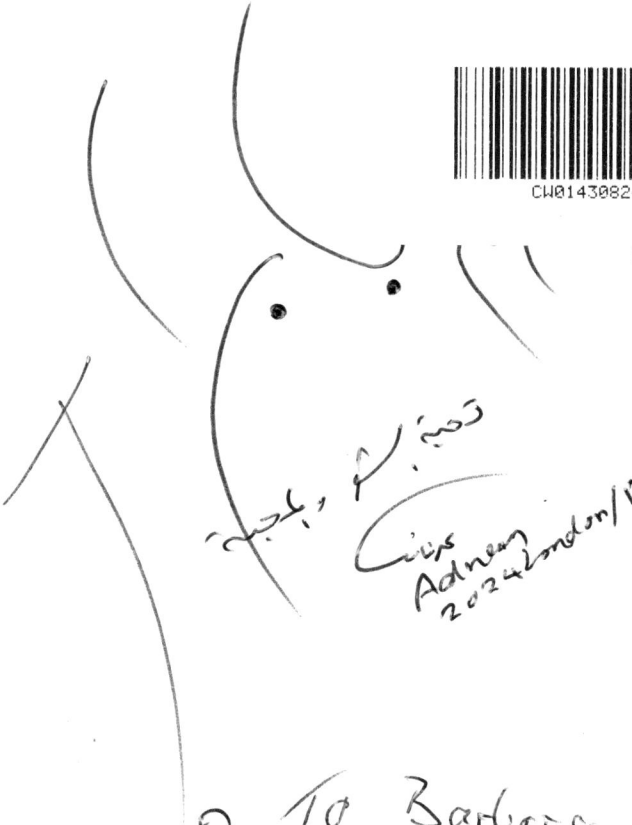

CW01430824

Cuss
Adnan
2024 London/Baghdad

O To Barbara

Love

Adnan. Valerie x

To cuddle my exile..

To cuddle my exile

Adnan al-Sayegh

Translated by: Jawad Wadi

Edited and proof read by:
V. Q. Phillips and J. Knight

To cuddle my exile
By: Adnan al-Sayegh
Translated by: Jawad Wadi
Edited and proof read by V. Q. Phillips & J. Knight
Front Cover. 'The Lane' by kind permission of Jenni Notton the artist.
Back Cover: Poem dedicated to Adnan by Abdul-Wahab Al-Bayati, (1926-1999), One of the modern poetry pioneers in Arabic.
(Derived from the diwan "book of elegies" by Albayati published by "The Arabic foundation for studies and publishing" Beirut 1995. The poem was issued in "Alwihda "Unity" magazine) No 82-83, July, August 1991 Paris).
Cover design by Dana Al-Zubaidi

Printed and bound in Great Britain by
Imprint Digital, Upton Pyne, Exeter

ISBN: 978-1-908853-99-8

Published by Ink Lines, an imprint of Valley Press
Woodend, The Crescent, Scarborough, YO11 2PW

I would like to give special thanks to Saadi Abd Al-Latif, Claire C. Dobson, Marga Burgui-Artajo, Dr. Salah Niazi, Dr. Hassan Abdulrazzak, Rita Odeh, Dr. Abbas Kadhim, Soheil Najm, Dr. Salih J. Altoma, Dr. Ali Al-Manna and Yasmin Ahammad. Without their meticulous editing, the work would not have been accomplished

Contents

The title of this book stems from "Ta'bbata Manfa"which in Arabic means "Exile under his armpit", a wordplay on a name of a very famous poet in the Pre-Islamic period "Ta'abbata Sharran".

It is an old anecdote in which the mother of the poet had been asked about her son, and where he could be found. She did not give a straight forward answer. Instead she said Ta'abbata Sharran. She meant that he had concealed a knife under his armpit, to commit a crime. The son was, thereafter, a vagabond poet (Su'luk) to be known as Ta'abbata Sharran who died approximately in 530 A.D.

Introduction

In the 18th century William Blake was quoted as saying, 'Cast aside from poetry all that is not inspiration'...1. The ingenious poetry of **Adnan Al-Sayegh** will not be cast aside, for each sentence, stanza and momentary silence is filled with inspiration. It is the inspirational that enables the reader to empathize with, yet transcend, the palpable sense of loss and sadness inherent in many of his poems.

> *What's happening to me?......(1)*
> *Meanwhile my homeland was away in*
> *an exile distance....(2)*
> *I have nothing*
> *But this snow.....(3)*

Harrowing lines such as these create an awareness of Adnan's perturbing history, whilst actually underscoring it.

Adnan al-Sayegh was born in Al-Kufa Iraq in 1955. Since his early childhood until this day, Adnan has had an insatiable appetite for reading. The outcome being, that he is erudite about the works and experiences of poets and writers from around the world, be they ancient or modern. The first poem that he wrote was a sensitive verse about his terminally ill father, Adnan was then 10years old. Today he is one of the most original voices of the Iraqi poets who came to prominence in the 1980s. Against his will Adnan, along with other young men was forcibly conscripted into the Iraqi Army. Resistance would risk execution. As a result he saw combat in the 1980-

1989 Iraq - Iran war, and it was during this cataclysmic conflict that Adnan was detained for reading unauthorized books as the authorities had forbidden this activity. "You are supposed to fight not read" was their polemic. In 1984 along with other imprisoned men, he was confined in an abandoned animal stable, situated on the borders of Iraq and Iran.

Not only was the stable used as an arsenal for boxes of dynamite, but beyond the perimeters of barbed wire the ground was strewn with hidden land- mines. To make the situation even more horrific, there was the threat of being killed by the frequent bombing raids. Alarmingly, one of his fellow prisoners who suffered from schizophrenia, insisted on brewing his tea inside the stable close to the boxes of dynamite. The smell of stale dung, by comparison, paled into insignificance. Suffice to say that Adnan was physically bound and incarcerated in dangerous and appalling conditions. Mentally however it was not so. A phrase written by the poet John Milton in Comus, is more than apt. 'Thou canst not touch the freedom of my mind'... 2 Not only was the mind of Adnan free, it was poetically fertile. This impelled him, albeit surreptitiously and by candle light, to create poetry in which he fervently denounces the devastation of war and the horrors of dictatorship.

> *The Sultan transformed me into a soldier pawn*
> *In a war I did not grasp...*
> *I rebelled and*
> *Castrated soldiers took me blind-folded*
> *To the firing wall*
> *And directed their rifles*
> *Towards me....(4)*

Visually and verbally Adnan does not spare the reader. His words present with some force the parlous experience of his life during that time of conflict.

After his release in 1986 after serving his two years sentence Adnan, was
compelled to complete his service in the army. A newspaper editor who appreciated Adnan's literary skills employed him as a journalist. However, he continued to vehemently denounce the injustice and oppression of the ruling regime in his poetry. A section from a draft of his poem Uruk's Anthem, was adapted for the theatre and in 1993 it was performed at the Al Rasheed theatre in Bagdad. Uruk's Anthem is one of the longest poems in Arabic literature and eloquently articulates the deep despair of the subjugated people of Iraq. As a consequence of the play, rumours reached Adnan that his life was in danger. So in July of that year he fled Iraq to live in Jordan. On receipt of further threats he again took flight, this time for Beirut in 1996. It was there that the length of Uruk's Athem was published. This so enraged Sadam Hussein's son Uday that he condemned Adnan to death *(The death list was published in the newspaper "Babel" on the 13th of October 1996, then in "Al- Zawraa" on the "2rd of March 2000. Both these newspapers were owned by Uday)* To save his life, Adnan had to flee from Beirut, and after a circuitous and emotional journey he found, via the United Nations, refuge in Sweden. It was in Sweden that extracts of Uruk's Anthem, together with the poems of Nobel Laureate (2011) Tomas Tranströmer, formed a play which was performed in 2006, 2007, 2008 and 2014 as well as in Egypt 2007 and 2008. It was also performed in Morroco 2006, 2007, 2008 and 2014. Since 2004 Adnan has been living in exile in London.

So far I have quoted the words of two famous poets. I wish now to introduce my third, as not only is it relevant, it is also prophetic.

> 'The power of my pen will overcome the power of their bullets.'

I am quoting Adnan Al-Sayegh! He and his pen, like the Phoenix, have risen to overcome adversity and emerge as victors. He has used words as a weapon to condemn the ravages of war and the horrors of dictatorship; whilst the power of his pen has given him poetic permission to 'overcome the power of their bullets' and reach beyond the political and religious extremism that has caused him so much anguish. This allowed him to embrace, by using a lighter stroke of his pen, a poetic vision which encompasses the balance and beauty of the natural world.

> 'The islands are sea stumbles running towards the shore, Thus sea's losses
> Glitter far away.'........ (5)

With elegance and ease he has transported the reader from darkness into light and from the sinister to smiles. The tension and tightness in his writing has dissolved. Adnan is not burdened by 'carrying crosses' (6). Like the 'bird' in the poem 'Freedom,' Adnan and his poetry have flown 'far away' into the realms of nature, peace and tranquillity.

Using a sensitive yet precise directness, Adnan also has the ability to arouse both the readers' smiles and sensuality.

Without your lips
I don't know
how to pick the flower.......(7)

She makes love
As if she learnt it
By heart........(8)

She sits across from me in the library
spreading her legs
and I read between the lines.........(9)

In these succinct poems Adnan may be economical with his words, but there is no tight budget for our feelings. The impact is seductive and emotionally stimulating. These evocative lines whilst being alluring, also depict a sense of longing and loss. They reveal the personal turmoil that Adnan the man was unable to release whilst confined by the barbed wire and bullets. Adnan the poet however was liberated, able to find expression through release of the written word onto the page.

Adnan's written word on the page is reminiscent of the author Henry Fielding, but in a less intrusive manner. Unlike Fielding, Adnan does not engage in a leisurely preamble with his readers, nor does he tease them about 'Taking a nap' whilst reading his words...3 There is a sense of Adnan, sometimes tangible sometimes not, reminding the reader that they are reading poetry and that he is the poet. This sense of self in many poems is achieved by allowing the speaker of the poem to be identified in the first person. "Lulea", "The Second Shadow" and "Ghosts" are prime examples of this, as is the concise title "A Poet", a poem dedicated to the martyred poet Ali Al- Rammahi.

Still in control of the readers' emotions, Adnan lightens the mood with "The Bird of Poetry", whilst in "Only for Them" he directs us 'From a pub to a poem'…. The incongruity of these words are a joy to read. In addition, encompassed in some poems are references to the component parts of his creative craft. This is deftly communicated to the reader in the poem "Whiteness," where

'The censor in the book
Remains devouring the words
The lines, the letters
And the commas.
Until he gets a fat belly
From eating too many pages,…' ………(10)

The lexical term 'fat belly' creates not only a very vivid image of the 'censor', but it is also an excellent example of how Adnan intersperses his poetic language with what William Wordsworth called 'the very language of men'….4 It is in "The Poet" that Adnan reminds the reader that poetry is compiled by using 'Alphabet letters'. It is these very 'letters' that Adnan shapes and sharpens into his written word, so inflamed with Adnan's passion for justice, love and freedom that they almost scorch the page!

There have been many accolades and awards given to Adnan, a full list of which appears in this book. However, one such accolade is in the form of an MA thesis, written by Sura-Hussein-Mohammed Ali. This is a Psychological Study, in which she compares selected war poems by Adnan and Wilfred Owen. Both shared the experience of fighting in barbaric wars, both were able under severe distress to continue writing their poetry, in order that the world should know the truth about man's inhumanity to man. Owen penned a phrase which I dedicate to Adnan - 'All a poet can do today is warn. That is why the true poets must be truthful '...5

Adnan is a poet who despite appalling difficulties, still upholds the courage of his convictions, that mankind and nations who have been divided through the terrors of war and dictatorship will one day be united by a bond of fellowship, freedom and peace. This is the reason why his voice must continue to be heard over the 'higher minarets'; to reach those people who are 'hungry' for his words of encouragement and hope.(10) They will then realise that not only is he speaking the language of love, freedom and peace, but that the language he is speaking is truthful. The most meritorious and significant accolade which could be given is to call Adnan al-Sayegh a 'True Poet'.

References For Adnan's Poetry.
(1) Lulea. From "To Cuddle My Exile" (Sweden, 2001; Cairo, 2006).
(2) The Second Shadow. Ibid.
(3) Lulea. Ibid.
(4) Pawns. Ibid.
(5) Formations (No 7). Ibid.
(6) A Poet. Ibid.
(7) Formations (No 8). Ibid.
(8) Formations (No 9). Ibid.
(9) Variations. From "Under a Strange Sky", 1994 London; 2002 Beirut ; 2006 Cairo.
(10) Formations (No 6). From "To Cuddle My Exile".

Literary References.
1 "Milton a Poem". William Blake 1804-1811 p357 British Museum, Dept of Prints and Drawings London
2 "Comus. A Masque". John Milton. 1634 Line 664.
3 "Preface to Lyrical Ballads". 1802. William Wordsworth The Major Works including The Prelude. p 596 - 597.
4 Wilfred Owen Draft Preface. Prepared for a collection of war poems that he hoped to publish in 1919. Written in Ripon Yorkshire 1918.

International Awards:
1. Hellman-Hammett International Poetry Award.
   (New York 1996)
2. Rotterdam International Poetry Award. (1997)
3. Swedish Writers Association Award. (2005)

International Accolades:
1. A Master of Arts Thesis. "The Poetry of Adnan Al-Sayegh. A Technical Study" Submitted by Arif Al- Saadi. It was awarded a distinction by the Department of Arabic Language at the University of Al- Mustansiriyah Bagdad, 2006.
2. David Sullivan, Professor of English at Cabrillo College California USA. Introduced Adnan's poetry to the curriculum in 2011.
3. A Master of Arts Thesis. "Poem everyday life in the poetry of Adnan Al-Sayegh" Submitted by Ahmed Mohammed Ali. It was awarded a distinction by the Department of Arabic Literature at the University of Al- Mosul, 2011.
4. A Master of Arts Thesis. A Comparative Study of Selected War Poems by Wilfred Owen and Adnan Al-Sayegh. A Psychological Study. Submitted by Sura- Hussein- Mohammed Ali. It was awarded a competent degree pass by the College of Education for Women - The Department of English at The University of Bagdad, 2014.
5. A Master of Arts Thesis "Formation of Power in Adnan Al-Sayegh's Poetry" by Wassan Al-Jubouri. It was awarded a distinction by the College of Education for Women - Department of Arabic, at The University of Bagdad, 2015.
6. Emma Sky O B E, was the representative of the Coalition Provisional Authority in Kirkuk Iraq 2003 and then the political advisor to General Odierno US Army 2007-2010. She is also a Senior Fellow at Yale University's Jackson Institute, New Haven Connecticut U S A. In her latest book The Unravelling, Emma has included in her preface a poem written by Adnan called simply yet significant 'Iraq'.

Adnan is a member of the Iraqi and Arab writers Unions, the Iraqi and Arab Journalists Unions, the International Journalist Organization, the Swedish Writers Union, the Swedish Pen Club and Pen International England.

Listed below are some of various national and international venues and festivals where Adnan has read his poetry:

National.
- The Poetry Café - London 2009, 2012, 2014, 2014, 2015.
- Britain's National Poetry Day - London 2009.
- White Chapel Gallery - London 2009.
- Exiled Writers Ink - London 2009, 2011, 2012.
- Tonight Poetry of Exile – Portsmouth 2009 and Petersfield Write Angle poetry- Petersfield 2010 Britain.
- Millennium Centre - Cardiff, Wales, Britain 2010.
- Al- Kufa Gallery 2000, 2005, Iraqi Society 2004, 2005 and Iraqi Cultural Centre 2012, 2013, 2014, The Humanitarian Dialogue Foundation 2010, 2011 and Poems to Al-Mutanabbi Street - London 2013, 2015.
- SOAS University - London 2010, 2011, 2012.
- The University of Cambridge, Britain 2011.
- StAnza Scotland's International Poetry Festival St Andrews, Edinburgh - Britain 2011.
- Contemporary Arts Centre - Glasgow, 2011.
- The National Portrait Gallery - London 2011.
- William Blake festival - London 2011, 2012.
- The University of Leeds - Britain 2012.
- The Royal Academy - London 2012.
- Imperial College 2013, William Goodenough College 2013 and The Goldsmith University of London - London 2015.
- The University of Oxford, Britain 2013, 2014.
- The Ashmolean Museum - Oxford, Britain 2013, 2014
- The British Museum - London 2014.
- Keats House - London 2014.
- The Poetry International Festivals with English PEN Writers at South Bank Centre - London 2015.
- The University Of Manchester – Department Of Arts, Languages and Cultures - Manchester, Britain 2013, 2015.

International.
- Poetic 'Nation' Festival, Baghdad 1984 and the General Union of Iraqis Writers Baghdad – Iraq 1984, 1987, 1992, 1993, 2004.
- Baghdad Arts Academy 1986, University of Basra 1989, 1993, University of Mosul 1988, 1993, Al-Anbar University 1992 and University of Literature Baghdad – Iraq 1990.
- Babylon International Festival 1987 and in the temple of Nanmaj in the ancient city of Babylon - Iraq 1992.
- Al- Marbid poetic Festival Baghdad and Busra 1988, 1989, 2006 and Al Mada Cultural Week Festival, Erbil - Iraq 2007.

- *Poetry Festival Cairo 1990, 2003, The Alexandria Library - Alexandria 2003 and Cairo International Book Fair, Cairo - Egypt 2007.*
- *XII Jerash Festival Amman – Jordan 1993.*
- *Literature Festival in University of Sana'a and The Writer's Union of Aden - Yemen 1993.*
- *Arabic poetry festival, Khartoum – Sudan 1995 .*
- *Cultural Forum, Beirut – Lebanon 1996.*
- *International Poetry Festival in Rotterdam - Holland 1997.*
- *International Poetry Days Festival, Malmo - Sweden 1997.*
- *International of World Book Day in Malmo 2000, Malmo annual World Festival 2001, 2005 and Festival of World Book Day, Christianstad – Sweden 2010.*
- *The Writer's Union, Oslo 2000 and The World Book Day Festival, Oslo – Norway 2001.*
- *Arab and Danish Culture Festival, Copenhagen - Denmark 1999, 2000.*
- *Iraqi Al Raphidian Cultural Festival Days, Berlin 2000, 2008, 2010 and Iraqi human rights associations, Berlin - Germany 2014.*
- *The Arab Cultural Centre, Damascus – Syria 2002.*
- *Doha Cultural Festival, Qatar 2002.*
- *Kuwait Forum first Iraqi Poetry 2005 and The Kuwait International Book Fair - Kuwait 2011.*
- *International Poetry Festival, Medellin - Colombia 2005.*
- *Nights of poetry, Bari - Italy 2007.*
- *Arab Cultural Festival, Muscat - Oman 2008, 2010, 2012, 2014.*
- *Arab Cultural Club in Sharjah 2008 and Abu Dhabi International Book Fair – UAE 2014.*
- *The Tunisian House of Poetry, Tunisia 2008.*
- *Festival of Arab Heritage Toronto, Calgary – Canada 2008.*
- *Michigan State University - USA 2008.*
- *International Poetry Festival, Morocco 2009, 2010, 2012, 2013, 2014, 2015.*
- *Al Jawahiry Centre - Prague 2009.*
- *International Poetry Festival, Havana - Cuba 2009.*
- *Strokestown International Festival, Dublin - Ireland 2010.*
- *Cafe "cultural Havana" in Mecca 2010 and International Poetry Festival, Riyadh, Dammam - Saudi Arabia 2014.*
- *Museum of Mahmoud Darwish, Ramallah - Palestine 2014.*
- *Festival International, Ecuador - South America 2014.*
- *Al- Kufa University, Al- Kufa 2015 and The University of Baghdad, Baghdad - Iraq 2015.*
- *Circulo Intercultural Hispano Arab, Madrid - Spain 2015.*
- *The University Of Tokyo – Department Of Languages, Tokyo - Japan 2015.*
- *L'Harmattan Arts et Cultures - Paris France 2016.*

The following collections of Adnan's poetry have been published:

1. Wait for me under the Statue of Liberty (Bagdad, 1984).
2. Songs on the Bridge of Kufa (Bagdad, 1986; Cairo, 2011).
3. Sparrows don't Love Bullets (Bagdad, 1986).
4. Sky in a Helmet (Bagdad, 1988; Cairo 1991 and 1996)
5. Mirrors for her Long Hair (Bagdad, 1992; Amman & Madrid, 2002).
6. Cloud of Glue (Bagdad, 1993; Damascus, 1994; Cairo 2004).
7. Under a Strange Sky (London, 1994; Beirut 2002; Cairo, 2006).
8. Formations (Beirut and Amman, 1996).
9. Uruk's Anthem (Beirut, 1996 and 2006).
10. To Cuddle My Exile (Sweden, 2001; Cairo, 2006; Baghdad, 2015).
11. And.. (Beirut, 2011; Baghdad, 2015).

In other languages:
1. Att Bära Sin Exil (Swedish & Arabic), translated by a number of translators, overseen by Arne Zaring, (Sweden, 2010).
2. The Deleted Part (English), translated by Stephen Watts and Marga Burgui-Artajo, (United Kingdom, 2009).
3. Nagelskrift (Swedish), translated by Bodil Greek and Staffan Wieslander (Sweden, 1998 and 2000).
4. Selections (Dutch), translated by Jaco Schoonhoven, (Netherlands, 1997).
5. Bajo Un Cielo Extranjero (Spanish), translated by Abdul H. Sadoun and Muhisin Al-Ramly (Spain, 1997).
6. Bombs Have Not Breakfasted Yet (English), translated by Dr. Abbas Kadhim and David Sullivan, (United Kingdom, 2013).
7. The poet who does not reach his letters to his homeland (Farsi), selected poems, translated by Mohammad Mehdi Nzad (Iran - Tehran, 2014).
8. Now as Then: Mesopotamia-Iraq (English and Arabic) by Jenny Lewis and Adnan Al-Sayegh, (United Kingdom, 2013).
9. Singing for Inanna (English and Arabic) by Jenny Lewis and Adnan Al-Sayegh (United Kingdom, 2014).
10. ''Le sommet est un puits'' (French) The top is an over turned well, selected poems, translated by Dr. Mohamed Salah Ben Amor (France, 2015).

And his Poetry has been translated into other languages such as: French, Italian, German, Romanian, Norwegian, Danish, Dutch and Kurdish.

By V. Q Phillips. BA.

Premonitions

The tiniest knock on the door…
Confused I hid my poems
In the drawers
The frequent
Knockings are like an echo
Of police patrolling
In the streets
Of my head.
Nevertheless
I know for sure that one day
They will knock on my door
Their trained fingers
Like police dogs will
Reach the drawers
Of my heart
And pluck out my papers
And……..
My life…..
To depart later
Peacefully.

Beirut, Lebanon, 1 October 1996

(.......!!)

Oh! My God
Is it true?
That those tyrants
passed through
Your translucent fingers
And you endured them!!?

Malmö, Sweden 1999

A Homeland Tale

When the statue of Mr President
Felt bored
He descended from his golden pedestal
Leaving behind the delegations, the blossoms and the
Children's chants.
He began walking between the people
Who rushed up to him applauding and shouting,
"With our souls with our blood we sacrifice Ourselves
to you"
The statue felt invigorated.
When his other statues heard this
They stepped into the squares
And started fighting each other
The people as they watched, began to wonder
Which of them was Mr President.....?

Malmo, 1999

"No"

For the story-writer Hamid Al-Moukhtar

His mouth
Which used to say "No"
They rolled into dust.
Numerous trees then grew over the length of the land
The Emperor heard their rustles
When they passed his palace's windows
As if they were the bells of "No's"

Malmo, 25 October, 1999

Ghosts

I am used to constantly hearing unfamiliar voices
Mindlessly chanting my name
Then their iron steps ascending the stairs
To place their grips on the door
Their muzzles are pointing at my temple
Leaving my corpse rolling
Behind the roaring of their cars' engines
The people clamour together wondering
-Where did they come from?
-But they did not come
All that was left for me was an open scene
As wide as the postponed bullet.

Khartoum, 26 December, 1995

Parties

Signboards marching
Amid a jungle of slogans
They started disputing about
Who should be the first to march

First they fought with their hands
Then with cudgels

Afterwards...
The signboards fell down

And we who were crowded on both sides of the road
Could not see anything but
A jungle of interlocked rifles
Marching towards us...

Lulea, Sweden, 14 January 1997

A Door

I see them
pushing me to come in
pushing me to get out
Behind them there is slamming in my ribs
But no one turns around
To see
How exhausting and
How inferior
The role of a door is!

Cosia Hotel Praque, 3 July, 1999

Altitude

Whenever the dog barks
Behind the cloud
It passes him by
And never heeds
The waggery

Lulea, 25 December, 1996

Threads

Alone she sits
Before the window
Knitting the wool,
A lonely passer -by
Pulls the threads
Pulls the woman.
Inserting his needle in
He remains knitting
Thus they weave their dreams
Every day
And between them

A whispering thread…
That never arrives.

Modca Café Beirut, 16 March 1996

Frustrations

I wait for the barren branches
To blossom
And for the furled banners
To unfurl
but when the roses bloomed
Other than me who picked them?
When the banners marched
they left me on the pavement
They went on pushing their way
Amid the roaring…
Towards the palace courtyard.
I waited until the sailing ships returned
But as the sailors and passengers came down
I did not find
Any one who could recognize me
I knocked on all the cells
Until they were opened
But as soon as the prisoners got out
Opening their arms and lungs
Towards freedom
They dragged me by my arms
And forcefully locked me
Inside a cell.

Damascus, Syria 3 March, 1996

If

If once
The cudgels and whips
Return to the fields,
To re-enact the wailings of bodies
That were severed by their stings.
The trees would bury their limbs alive
And the forest would go on hunger strike.
Then
There would no nightingales
Or branches

Outside the Ferdan prison, Beirut, 16 October 1996

Siege

Floundering with our fins
Through water folds
The air is suffocating us
And those sitting
Before the glass
Of our elegant tank
Look with pleasure
At our gasping breath
Shattering the haze
Searching for scraps of air
We
The Fish
Besieged
Inside our homeland tank

Malmo, 1998

Whiteness

The censor who is in the book
Remains devouring the words
The lines, the letters
And the commas
Until he gets a fat belly
From eating too many pages
Then he disappeared
Oh! My God
What am I going to do
With such whiteness?
The whiteness is but a veil.

Lulea Library, Lulea 2 April 1997

A Meal

Hunger
Extends its claws
Into my belly
So I devour my papers
And walk away
I place my hand on my belly
In fear that someone
Would hear
The words grinding.

Hashemite Square, Amman, Jordan, Autumn 1995.

An Equation

To descend
Or to ascend
- No difference -
Wherever you roam…?
The top…
Is an over turned well.

Vasteras, Sweden, 4 December, 1999

An Elderly Shoemaker

Sitting
On the pavement
Before his box
He stares at his days
The people are putting on.

Damascus, Syria 1996

Geometry

The square
Sits cross legged
On a page settee
Sighing
O! Rectilinear
I could go with you to eternity
If they had not closed
My ribs around me

Malmo, 1997

A Gale

Distracted
By your departure
Like an eagle
Fluttering
In the face of a storm
While his feathers
Are scattered
Over the Steppes

Malmo, 1998

A Plea

Oh! My God
One life
Or even ten
Are not enough
To satisfy my desire for her sensuality
Grant her to me

Instead of your heavenly virgins
And Heavenly rivers,
Or am I free to choose

Beirut, 1996

A Poet

For the martyr, the poet Ali Al- Rammahi

In the era of the tyranny
Castrated poets
Shrink in the lap
Of the Sultan
Like rats-
Singing for his majesty glories
And his blessing.
But you with your
Alphabet letters
Remain walking
-Every time- Everywhere-
Carrying crosses
On your shoulders

Rawdha Café, Damascus, Syria, 8 March 1996

Only For Them

How much time,
Papers and pavements
Did they waste ?
Those who cursed at me in the festivals
In the lavatories
And in the newspapers.

Those who followed me
With secret reports
From a pub to a poem
From a homeland to exile
Carrying their secret reports
Those I feel pity for them now

Their hollow lives
Have nothing
But me.

The International Poetry Festival in The Netherlands, June 1997

Complex

The Fascists
And Castrated poets
Catch the two ends
Of a concluded rope

Around my neck

And....
Begin to tighten

Beirut, 7 September 1996

A Passer By

He neither opened
A window in a house
Nor planted flowers
In the palm of "If only"
He was never delighted
By neither a flute
Nor a verse
In his life
He passed as a shadow
You don't know
Whether he is dead or alive!!!

Malmo, 1999

Redundant Thoughts

I enter the lavatory
Thinking about the life cycle
I pull the Siphon
To wash away
The rotten thoughts
I get out free
As if our heads
Were in need of a W C

Lulea, 1996

Familiarity

He is dedicating himself
In his workshop
This elderly carpenter
Making coffins for people
He forgets
To think about his death
Familiarity deprives him
Of his feelings.

Khartoum, Sudan, 31 December 1995

Waterwheels

How long will you remain
Turning
And Turning?
Oh! Abdallah, the obscure
Like a horse of a waterwheel
Irrigating a land
That plants nothing for you
But a wasteland.

Al- Kufa, Iraq, 1988

A Bottle

He sits before me
Quaffing glasses
One after another
Until his depths
Brim and he flows
The waiters hastened
Complaining to wipe him
Away from tables,
The passages
And the people…
Was he a man
Or a bottle of wine?

Beirut, 15 May 1996

A Compass

The captain hesitates
Between the deck
And seabed
Considering
The World's winds
Were not suitable
For sailing

Freedom

Between the cage full with grain
And the barren horizon
The bird of poetry flaps his wings…
….. Far away
….. In the winds
And never hesitates

Copenhagen airport, 1998

A Folk Proverb

Ten people
Are farting in the house.
Oh! you Crazy
Why do you incense for them?

Dust

With no wings
The dust is flying
Mocking thousands
Of things
It left on the earth.
*

Oh! You the dust
No matter how
They raise you
You will definitely
Fall
To the floor
Quicker than your height
*

Why tied to earth
Does dust have a homeland?

Jönköping, Sweden, September 1999

Formations

(1)
Don't pick the rose
Look…
How proud it is of its short life
*

(2)
In the tiger's mind
Many preys
Are outside the bars of his cage
Being hunted by the liquid of his tongue
*

(3)
Inside the slaughtered soul
plenty of dancing,
But the body pivot
Is not wide enough
*

(4)
Now you are ashes,
It does not matter to me
That once you were embers
*

(5)
Oh you the faults
How many times
Did we insult you?
When you became useless
*

(6)
Whenever their minarets
Become higher
The hungry voice
Is less and less heard!
*

(7)
The Islands
Are sea stumbles
Running towards the shores
Thus
Sea's losses glitter far away
*

(8)
Without your lips
I don't know
How to pick the flower!
*

(9)
To reach there or not
What's the difference
When I don't find you
*

(10)
She makes love
As if she learnt it
By heart
*

(11)

There are no fingers anymore
On my hand to wave with
Since I used to bite them
Out of remorse

*

(12)

Do mirrors remember us
When we go away from them

*

(13)

I'll pick the flower
Pick it
But to whom will I give it
In this twilight moment
Of my solitude

*

(14)

Nobody is looking at anybody
Everybody is looking at each other

*

(15)

If your beauty had no hanger
Where would we hang
Our mistakes..?

*

(16)

Her beauty which she lived
Exceedingly
Has broken between
Her fingers.
And she could not stoop
To pick up the rest
Of her life.
*

(17)

It is the body's curse
To sleep alone,
On the embers
Satisfying with his fingers
Away from women
Seducing his dreams,
Leaving nothing
Just the foam.
*

(18)

As you passed by
With your apricot cheek
How many lips smacked for you
On your way to me?
*

(19)

With its watery needle
The rain is sewing
The shirt of fields
*

(20)
What do our shadows do
In the presence of light
*

(21)
Thus
We sit
Face to face
Our fingers are interlaced
While our hearts
Prepare suitcases
For leaving
*

Variations

(1)
The candle has no country
Out of it's darkness
*

(2)
Fish are abundant
My nets are torn
Oh, what a mean sea
*

(3)
He gets confused
To see the roundness of her buttocks

But he doesn't get confused
At the roundness of the universe
*

(4)
As long as speech stretches
……. It vanishes.
*

(5)
Our feet…
Are moving pavements.
*

(6)
The feet …
Which walk
In all directions…
Never arrive
*

(7)
In the coal there is
Imprisoned fire…
*

(8)
The wall is asking
About the sense of the window
*

(9)
The shadow
Is the aging of time
*

(10)
The wheel's spinning
Is the place's repetition
*

(11)
Speech is
An internal running
*

Raouches Pigeons Rock - Beirut 1996

Pawns

The Sultan transformed me
Into a soldier pawn
In a war I did not grasp
To defend a chessboard.
I don't know whether it is
A homeland or a ring
So I rebelled
But the castrated soldiers
Took me blind folded
To the firing wall
And directed the barrels
Towards me.
I cried: "Stop"
Telling them
You will be dragged
To this square
One by one
Like rams,
And the crowns
Will rise
Upon the ladder of your broken bodies.

To...

He who was my dear friend
Before we separated
And amid the melancholy of the poem
He who remained in the shadows shrinking
For fear of daylight and the road's remoteness.
I went to the sun
For I did not fear being burnt
Or wandering aimlessly
Among clouds of distant hopes
He who was my dear friend...
Minded nothing
But to follow me
In the narrow paths
Like my shadow
Only to curse me in the newspaper.

Autobiography of a Muffled Gun

(1)
On the way to his obscure task
Why does this elegant master
Polish me
Every morning?
*

(2)
My friend remains
To steal glances
At the face of a man
Behind the glass of a bookstore
He was turning over a book
Then suddenly saw
The trousered posterior
Of my friend
He is confused
Did I frighten him?
I asked my friend
He nudges me to be quiet.
The man's face pales
As he turns suddenly
And sees me
He left the book
Vanished quickly in the crowd
Leaving my friend
Looking for him furiously
*

(3)

Amidst the crowd of many necks
How will my master
Know his victim?
*

(4)

One evening
While it was raining heavily
In the town's streets
He took me out
Of his warm pocket
He moved me with coldness
Directed me
To a man's back
Who stops
To pick up something I cannot see
But the man stoops
Over the unseen thing
Then my compatriot
Beats a hasty retreat.
*

(5)

After years of working
I was infected with
A chronic disease.
So my friend
Took me to a shop
The owner was
A man stained with oil.
Frowning he stared at me for
A long time,
Regretfully
pursing his lips
And said with indifference

That I was no longer useful
For anyone, or anything.
So my friend callously left me.
Without realising
That one day
He will be thrown out
Just like me!
*

(6)
Among heaps of ribs
And iron limbs
I turned carefully around
To see stacks of colleagues
With different shapes and rattles.
We talked before sleep
About the night patrols
We used to do
When we caused blindness
In their eyes and hearts
The necks we used to see so proud
We wondered why suddenly
Such necks shivered
Like spikes that were bent
By the winds of tyranny-
While we were laughing
About our wide ranging life
Which ….
Meant nothing
But just a cocked trigger.

Malmo, 15 July, 1997

The Venerable God

He was concerned
By the numerous complaints
The angels delivered
To him angrily
And the tears that reached
His post box
Withered and filthy
As well as the curses
Upon him daily
With or without reason.
He wanted to know
What was happening
In our country
So disguised
In rustic clothes
He descended
From his splendid heaven
To wander in the streets
Of the town
He was amazed to see
Photos of Mr President
Filling out
The walls, the air
And the T. V. screens
The imposing convoy
Of Mr president passed jingling
-Amid a chorus of clappers, signboards and the guardians-
The cheers rose up
From the mouths of zealous pavements
And the buildings
The trees, the people
And the clouds began to dance
Suddenly
Someone nudged the venerable god

And fearfully said to him
Oh! You idiot clap!
Otherwise, his rough guards
Will drag you away.

Malmo, 15 July, 1997

The Second Shadow

I stood before the building
Confused
His shadow was following me
From behind the newspaper
It went around all the streets with me
He joined me at
A restaurant in the
Suburbs, to the bus
And adjacent bookstores
Even to the toilets.
I shared equally with him
My horror in the poem
Feeling its folds
Sticking through my shirt
My pulse began to beat quickly…
And the clash of hasty wheels
And kisses moving quickly behind the branches
He felt - while turning around -
His swollen back pocket
And I saw a muzzle
Lurking me
………..

However we didn't separate.
We crossed so many streets
And did not separate.
We passed by café's songs
As the flies alight on the melodies
And fly to the tea,
A lady in a short skirt
Coming down the bus stairs.
And the dubious glances pinched her thighs
And she got frightened,
The huge crowd surging
Upon the bank of shops

To ebb by the end of the month
Towards the houses,
To dry their days
On the debts of a clothes line.
The announcer lisped with "L"
When uttering the name of the Culture Minister,
The barmaid who
suffers from lack of sleep
The fountains
Of Beirut Square
And still we did not separate
....

As I entered the bar
He followed me
His claws reaching for my shadow
Mean while my homeland
Was away in an exile distance
And a cup of tea
He was reading in the daily papers
His latest news
Puffing out on the foggy glass
The smoke of his rolled cigarette
And spitting.....
[When I shake hands with him
He'll give me a hand amputated
By splinters,
He points...... (to the sarcastic executioner's photo
At the top of the page
Adorned with badges-
He has been puffed up by the papers!-
Adhesion follows him as do the crowd and the
cameras)..
I point out to the rain
Falling from the clouds of his cyelids
As he gazes at the hunger in his streets

And the buildings - stealthily feeling his tumours
Far from government's eyes,
Rising higher, higher and higher
Sucking his blood and getting higher...]
...Looking at the buses
Pushing each other
And the steps push each other...
...Where is this flock panting to?
I anxiously drank half a cup
We exchanged glances
I turned around
And saw who was watching me
Hidden behind his glasses
And my back, straining with his ears to the table's edge
We exchanged but short phrases.
What can this mouse of the government
Register to the ear of his friend?
To prepare - behind reports
And his leather coat -
His fatal shot

Hassan Ajmi Café, Bagdad, Late 1992

Luleå

I look at the snowy sky
Waving to me
As it disappeared behind the pines
Does it concern me that the pines
Are blanketed with sparrows
And fast kisses
Does it concern me that girls smoke their secrets
Behind the windows
Does it concern me that this land
has not been mutilated
By a gun for two centuries
Does it concern me that the sky which snowed
And then became sunny
. . . .
. . . .
Does it concern me
While I have no homeland
Only these steps,
As if my longing
Shortened or hastened them
As I pretend to be busy
With brighter business
Instead of what really worries me!
. . . .
I say to my heart where do I go?
They destroyed my country
And then pretended to cry for me

The patrols on the distant borders
Are looking at my face
Scarred by the tank chains.
Since morning they scrutinize my name
And then cast me aside
As if my homeland

Were sealed with inadvertent
Falling tears.
As if the police stations
Were revolving me
As if I were alone
In my dungeon
In the bar's corner
Gulping in one go
What has been left
For me
And then little by little
Fade away……..
………………..
I have nothing
But this snow
Shading my window and the trees,
Whenever the girl nearby
Asks me about my direction
The clouds interlace
Upon our tears
As we begin to cry.

At a pub in the South of the North Pole, 6 April, 1997

Passage To Exile

The train's wails awaken the tunnels' sadness
Storming along rails of long-lived memories
And I am nailed to the window
With half of my heart
And the other half left behind on the table
Playing poker with a young woman, her thighs half-
covered
And she asks me with pain and shock
Why my fingers are so lacerated
Like the wood of over-used coffins
Hasty as if afraid of not being able to hold on to
Anything.
I tell her about my homeland and the fluttering Banners
And colonisation
And the glories of the nation
And how to make love for the first time in the toilets.
Then she leans-her wet hair-over my tears without
understanding
And in the other corner
Mozart scatters his harmonies across moor lands
Wrapped in snow…
And my homeland is sadder than it should be
And my songs are defiant, wild and diffident
I will lay myself down on the first pavement I see in
Europe
And raise my legs up to the passers-by so that I will Show
Them the wheals of school beatings and detention Camps
Which made me come here
What I carry in my pockets is not a passport
But a history of oppression
Where for fifty years we've kept ruminating on Fodder
And speeches...
…And hand rolled fags…
As we stand before the gallows
Watching our dangling corpses gesticulating at us

And we applaud the rulers
....From fear of the dossiers on our families in the Secret
police vaults
Mean while the homeland begins and
The homeland ends
...With the speech of the president
And between all this the president's streets & the
President's songs& the president's
Museums &the president's bounteousness & the
President's trees & the president's factories &the
President's newspapers & the president's stables & The
president's clouds & the president's army camps & the
president's statues & the president's bakeries & the
president's medals & the president's Mistresses & the
president's schools & the President's farms & the
president's weather & the President's orders & ...
She will look at me for a long time
At my eyes wet with rains and spit
Then she will ask me where am I from?

A CRY AGAINST HUMANITY!
- Anti-War Poetry by Adnan Al –Sayegh -

A Comparative Study of his Selected War Poems, extracted from a Psychological Study, of Adnan Al-Sayegh and Wilfred Owen. This study was submitted in February 2014 by Sura Hussein Mohammed Ali, to The University of Baghdad, as a Thesis towards a Master of Arts degree in English Literature.
Supervised bY Assist. Prof. Hana' Khalief Ghani (Ph.D.)

Abstract

This paper aims at exploring the impact of the Iraq-Iran war in the poetry of Adnan Al-Sayegh. His participation in this war makes him a firsthand witness to the atrocities of the trenches and fighting in the front lines. This war did not only change his life and world view for good, it changed the nature of his poetry as well. As a result, war becomes a central issue not only in the poetry Al-Sayegh wrote in the 1980s and 1990s in Iraq, but also in exile.
Key Words: War Al-Sayegh Poetry.

In critically reading Adnan Al-Sayegh's (1955-) poetry which was written in Iraq, one must take into consideration that he was living in what he called "The Homeland of Wars". This description is not surprising since, in less than three decades, the Iraqis had been experiencing continuous wars that wreaked havoc in all aspects of life. Like other Iraqis, Al-Sayegh has had a firsthand experience of war atrocities and their tragic consequences. No doubt, these successive wars and their catastrophic occurrences left an indelible mark in the psyche of the Iraqis. However, nowhere is this impact clearer than in the poctry of Al-Sayegh which Ghalib Al- Shabinder asserts:
Raises the curtain on a more dangerous death than the physical; it is the moral and psychological death with which Al-Sayegh is concerned. This death reigns supreme over all aspects of life.

His poetry displays images of physical death, and trying to battle with the boredom of deadly routines. There is no attempt at hiding or beautifying what is already condemned in the war. But there is one subtle aspect which we must look for: the moral [and psychological] death.[1]

During the war, poetry for Al-Sayegh helped to alleviate the feelings of loss and frustration amidst the sounds of shelling and the overwhelming smell of death. Al-Sayegh's depiction of daily life in the trenches and front lines are realistic to the marrow. The images of the helpless and powerless soldiers who were forced to act deadly parts in the massive drama of war are vivid and very impressive. His poetry photographically captures the grotesque and gruesome experiences of war. He relies heavily on direct description, everyday language and all the figures of speech available to him, to present a war poem as close to reality as possible. This enabled Al-Sayegh, as Hatim Al- Sagar remarks, to "meet the war in the middle of the distance between the poem as a literary construction and himself as a poet/ soldier. He did this deliberately to make his poems closer to life and ordinary people".[2]

In the narration of his war experience, the soldier/ poet Al-Sayegh, assures his readers that "He has seen more trenches, camps, huts, and cannons than [them] / He has carried dozens of corpses away from the battlefields".[3] At the age of 26, Al-Sayegh found himself in a situation where "the absurdity of death intermingles with the absurdity of life".[4]

Al-Sayegh's poems photographically portrays the soldiers' daily life in the trenches and the frontlines ramparts; among the blown bodies of his friends and the smell of death. By making war his central cause and poetic concern, Al-Sayegh was able to acquire a socio-political vision that makes his poetry quite unique. Using poetry to denounce war and to defend his humaneness made Al-Sayegh's war poems "the closest to the spirit of the age and the most honest in translating his life experiences in all their varieties and dimensions".[5]

For Al-Sayegh, nothing is more real than the bombs, shells, and swollen corpses of the dead soldiers. Therefore, he admits in his poem 'Searching for an Address' that "*bombs do not lie/ as do the military leaders and their proclamations/ Then take all the bombs and describe the war/ Take all the bleedings of war/... And describe the peace in my country*". (370 L19-21)[6]

Al-Sayegh's treatment of war acquired new dimension in "Flowers For The New Morning". In this poem, he addressed the war directly. He was hopeful that sooner or later peace would come. He says: *"O war/ The swollen womb of life/ We planted everything inside you/ Our childhood and wishes, our poems, fears, and our anxious lifetimes/ So that on a dewy morning, You could beget/ the future child of peace"*. (394-5 L17-22)

Al-Sayegh acknowledged the inability to forget his war experience which accompanied him like his shadow. In the same poem, he wondered: *"How many bombs you have to count/ To declare the end of war/ How many flowers you have to pluck out / To shout 'O Spring!'/ O My heart!/ O the sparrow less city.../ How much sorrow you have to endure/ To write a poem of happiness"* (394 L8-16)

In his first diwan *'Wait For Me Under The Statue Of Liberty'* (1984), the realistic portrayal of war atrocities remained its most predominant theme. The opening lines of Al-Sayegh's "Good Morning O Camp!" are evocative yet at the same time deceptive. The soldiers are talking about the "rising of the sun and the spread of its rays;" images, which Tarad Al- Kubaisi believes, are some of the most beautiful and memorable in war poetry.[7]

The image of a group of ordinary soldiers who are busy unbinding "The plaits of [their] sweet-sun"(638 L5), and, then, scattering them "plait.. by plait/ into the wind",(638 L7-8) contrasts sharply with the image of the 'gun' that preceded it in the opening line. In this sense, the calmness of these lines is disrupted by the presence of one of the most conspicuous tools of war: the gun. Al-Sayegh writes:

The guns rises..
early before the sparrows.
We ran
over the dews and deliriums.
We unbind the plaits of our sweet-sun-
We scatter them..
Plait. by plait
into the wind
And when the corporal pours… the Morning milk into the cups
We share the bread..
and the cosy laughter (638 L1-11)

In his article, "Good Morning, O Poet!", Youssif Nimer Dhayab points out that usually:

the guns resound and do not wake up early. It is the soldiers who wake up before the sparrows not the guns. The bread stands for the fate of the present situation which all of the soldiers share as they share the warm laughter.[8]

Here Al-Sayegh makes use of the natural landscape in general, and of the sparrows in particular. The sparrows here are a symbol of freedom, of the poets whose voices were muffled by the loud sounds of guns. In this way, Al-Sayegh juxtaposes romantic images of Nature, with ghastly images of war to emphasize the beautiful and the wonderful that is lost for good during the war.

As a matter of fact, the war is conspicuously present even in the poems which were dedicated to his anonymous sweetheart 'M'. In these poems, the language of war mingles with the language of love and courtship:

It is the Earth…
A Rebellious bullet
A homeland … for the sparrows and the poor
A homeland whose pain and suffering.. the poets (share)   ('M..
And The Poem of the Earth' (655 L1,11-13)

The spatial and environmental impact of war is crystal clear in Al-Sayegh's love poems. In "A Song on Khalifan's Versants", in which Al-Sayegh expresses his deep love for his sweetheart, he reflects on the various stages of his life in which he geographically moves from his birth place Al Kufa in the south of Iraq, to the cataracts in the north where the front lines he was fighting in were then situated. Once again, the vocabularies of war paradoxically mingle with the vocabularies of love:

I imagine her…
leaning … on the terrace now,
And the light that infiltrates… through the branches of the bitter orange
As pearls fall
on her plaits,
She was reading about Khalifan versant.
In my anthology,

About Al-Zab river..
... She lets her tearful eyes
Run in Shaqlawah resorts.
She forgot her rose... and bag
In Bikhal
And hastens ... to meet me
O Al-Zab River!... slow down
And carry to my sweetheart-in Kufa- my longing
.... and my salaam (greeting) (654 L27-42)

In consequence of that, the war for Al-Sayegh was not a transitory or accidental occurrence. It was indeed, a daily recurrent event that hounded the mind and the soul of the poet. It penetrated into his memory and chased him where ever he went, from the versants of the mountains and waterfalls in the north, to the marshes in the south. His romantic interest in the natural landscapes and warm hearted humane feelings, cannot be separated from his interest in the particulars of the daily life in the camps and battle fields. The poems in Al-Sayegh's second anthology *Songs At Al-Kufa Bridge* (1986) echoes the themes, concerns and connotations of the first anthology; which glowed with the fires of the battles, to die away with the expectation of death by the next bullet shot.

Al-Sayegh's poetry at this stage of his poetic career was characterized, generally speaking, by a heavy reliance on prosaic narratives that makes use of dialogue and monologue, besides the frequent references to specific persons and events".[9] Those persons who were either martyrs, prisoners-of-war, ordinary soldiers, or missing, became the pivotal axis around which the poems revolved.

In "Two Stanzas from the Martyr Fadhel Al- Najafi's Life", Al-Sayegh lodges a complaint and gives vent to his sorrows and concerns. He addresses his friends, reminding them of the happy moments in their lives. He says:

Do you remember?
You would feel absolutely desolate
If your sweetheart ever quarrelled with you.
You dream of her hair scattered
In the stations,
And along the ramparts,
....

But you are now nearby the ramparts
(Motionless, widower, and lonely discarded)
You are deeply resentful of the bullet
That disappointed you..
That faded away without a glimmer! (562 L37-47)

Noteworthy here is Al-Sayegh's tendency to interlace the images of love and craving, with the images of the insensitive and savage war. Amidst the scenes of death and desperation, the motionless, discarded corpse of his comrade-in-arms came to the fore to remind the readers of the ugliness and ghastliness of war.

In his third anthology *The Sparrows Do Not Love Bullets* (1986), al-Sayegh made use of the same images and techniques. The opening lines describe the beauty and splendour of the forest where a nightingale flew and sang tunefully by night as well as by day. A shot mercilessly assassinated the nightingale, turning it into a corpse. This incessant emphasis on sparrows and nightingales is purposeful since they stand for the beauty of nature, freedom, and inner peace which were slowly drained away from the poet's life. Interlacing these symbols with the fearful symbols of war such as shot, corpse and bullet; might betoken Al-Sayegh's deep and repressed desire to free himself from the shackles of war that put constraint on his ability to express himself freely. The last lines of his short poem 'A shot,' informs us of the death of all the nightingales. They were silenced for good. The metaphoric use of these nightingales opens the poem for various interpretations. They might stand for all the poets who, like Al-Sayegh, strongly objected to the war, or the soldiers and the Iraqis who were all forced to participate in this war. Al-Sayegh says: *"Swaying, the nightingale is busy singing tunefully/ a shot/ a corpse.../ the branch stands still...trembling/ For a moment/ Then falls motionless/All the nightingales/ Are put to silence in the Forest."* [465 L3-10]

In the other poems of the anthology which is famous for its reference to quiet landscapes and forests, Al-Sayegh mocks the war and challenges it to kill the beauty in his heart. In spite of the cruelty and the destructive nature of war, there is still enough room for love and poetry in Al-Sayegh's heart. In "Death Of A Shot", he writes:

I know quite well
The bullet is so damn cruel.
It shows no mercy.
But I challenge it.
I wrench away of my heart
The love poem,
Born this morning
At the door of the military post.
I challenge it
To silence the twittering of the
Sparrows of dawn
In the forest of my soul. [484-5 L1…34]

Al-Sayegh insists on the use of the vocabularies of love, beauty and hopefulness side by side with the vocabularies of war even in his poetry. Despite heavy fighting, he is always in search of the flowers that bloom in the mornings. He is always looking forward to the future, for a new life full of peace, joy and prospects.

In the same poem Al-Sayegh hopes that flowers will germinate in the versants which are a site of military operation. Probably, this poem was written after heavy shelling on the military post that he was in. This was Al-Sayegh's chosen method to overcome the violence and cruelty of life in the battlefields: to hope for a better future, to have flowers instead of shells and bullets. This is a well-known method which people often resort to in times of crises. In this way, Al-Sayegh seems to look for a way to psychologically treat his war traumas and his heart-breaks caused by the arbitrary death of people in the war.

In fact, Al-Sayegh can not help but extensively employ images of war, death, and frustration side by side with the images of friendship, love, family life and intimate chats. War becomes part and parcel of the Iraqis' daily life. As Al- Masri explains:

War, as an event that is rooted in reality, never sets Al-Sayegh's mind at ease or at rest. It never relieves his worries and fears. On the contrary, it always makes him worried, restless, confused and ill at ease. It always puts him in front of a new set of problems and complexities, which pave the way for new and contradictory possibilities such as victory and defeat. Death in its active or negative forms, i.e., either to kill or be killed, the physical and psychological wounds, blood shedding and a series of other dreary and tenebrous images.[10]

Al-Sayegh says

'Waiting the returning dead
and the death carriages
Distribute themselves among
the friends. ['The Bombs Mail' 435 L26, 32-34]

Al-Sayegh goes further to seek the assistance of the homeland and the safe house from which he was forcibly pulled out. Once again, he compares himself by extension to other soldiers and to the birds that were coercively taken away from their nests. He deeply regrets that his country was lost to war and destruction. In "War has no Name", Al-Sayegh is fully aware of the destructive and savage nature of war:

The war will cut the hand of our childhood
It starves us to death.
But we contend stubbornly
For the sake of our homeland.
It disperses and breaks up
Our days.
But we spend its days in
Entertaining hopes.
And we, the birds of longing
And love,
Seek the help of our sorrows' rests.
We shall cry over a (homeland)
Which they ruin.
So are we [452 L 21- 34]

The words in Al-Sayegh's poem are illustrative of the tears that betoken a deep sorrow that the poet feels for his homeland, which was ruined as a result of war. In the same poem he says:

There, where the soldiers sleep on
The coverlets of the wetted
Nostalgia,
The fragments of our expectations
Of a new day. [452 L5-9]

This feeling of hope and nostalgia was Al-Sayegh's main means to escape the pressures of daily life in the trenches. The juxtaposition of flagrant contradictions in the poem such as 'new day' which connotes hope and zealousness for life; and the 'menstruation' which implies blood shedding and death. This is indicative of the poet's psyche, which is torn to shreds between his desire to survive the war and his realisation of its mocking absurdity. The bread and the tea which are "essential ingredients in the Iraqi traditional meals" are indicative of Al-Sayegh's tendency to put the contraries together. Images of survival are side by side with images of death, images of desperation with images of hope and the dark colour of blood with the colour of a shining sun. This use of binary oppositions to spotlight what Al-Sayegh has already lost as a result of war, is one of the main characteristics that distinguishes him from other war poets.

The reader may wonder why Al-Sayegh, chooses to make the bread which the soldiers "divide among [themselves]" 'pierced'. In fact, the adjectives 'pierced', 'punctured' and 'perforated', recurrently appear in Al-Sayegh's poetry, particularly in this diwan in which they acquire great significance. The image of the 'pierced bread' is borrowed from the holes which the shots cause in the bodies of the soldiers.

The opening lines of the anthology tell of a hole in the soldier/ poet's lung, which is a miniature and metaphorical hole that stands for all the holes in the fabric of his own country. In "First Inaugurated," Al-Sayegh writes:

A helmet falls down...
I grope for the hole it makes in my lungs.
My palm was full of ashes.
A helmet falls down...
I grope for the hole it makes in my homeland.
I and it (my homeland)
Became chocked with the
Gushing blood. [423 L 7-14]

The 'pierced helmet' here stands for the poet's homeland which is likewise, pierced and destroyed. The holes in both the helmet and the poet's lung become like windows through which Al-Sayegh looks at both the sky and his country. In *A Sky In a Helmet* (1988), he addresses the sky saying: *"O Sky of Iraq.../ Is there no air/ The sky of Iraq was pierced with splinters"*. Even the sky of his homeland was pierced! [431-2 L44-46]

The poet cannot breathe not because of the hole in his lung, but because of the deep sorrow he feels for his country. He compares himself to a bird which, in spite of the spaciousness of the sky, cannot fly or move freely. The seven years of war which he spent in the battle fields are also full of holes. In "The Last Stations...The Beginning Of Madness", he says:

Sit down, pending my tears could catch breath
Pending my life could restore it's
lost years
(as if those years were seven minutes
not seven long years pierced with the madness
of my waiting) [428 L97-104]

The series of 'holes' continues to appear in the poem which the anthology is named after. In the same poem, Al-Sayegh tells:

The corporal says
It is death
Which neither accepts
So choose a hole for your head
As wide as your hopes
It is the time of holes... [430 L18- 24]

In this last line, Al-Sayegh sums up his idea of the war time in which his people are enduring. It is not only a 'hole' made by a shot. As a result, losing one's hopes of leading a normal life or enjoying it causes little surprise. His hopes now centre on his desire to physically survive the successive bullets shot at him and other soldiers. In this sense, the hole in Al-Sayegh's diwan performs an essential functional task. It is an expression of the downfall. It is the opposite of unity, coherence, repletion, and harmony. It is, in other words, a raped and violated time. There is neither peace nor hope. There are only horrendous holes through which we see, by which we breathe, and in which we live.[11]

The title of the anthology is the first thing that draws the attention of the reader. *A Sky In a Helmet* includes two similar and at the same time two different things. Just as the sky envelopes the earth completely, the helmet envelopes the soldier/ poet's head to protect it from possible injuries. However, this small helmet with its limited area has the ability to take in a whole sky. In other words, it became large or wide enough for the sky. In this sense, the wide and large is forcibly inserted into the small and narrow. This Al- Shabinder believes is not normal or even familiar. On the contrary, it is a portent of terrible things to come. This is exactly what Al-Sayegh wants to say. The war, in his poetry, is a colossal catastrophic and disruptive force.[12]

In this sense, his remarkable combination of two quite strikingly different things, is a sign of his awareness of the terrible affliction and suffering which his people are enduring. The sky as a symbol of hope, mercy and giving is, Al- Shabinder continues, sharply contrasted with the helmet as a symbol of war, distress, death and servitude of the soldier who is whining under its weight. The relationship between them becomes a relationship of life and death, war and peace. The wide sky fades away in the hole and is lost in the time of war.[13]Like the sky which becomes smaller and smaller until it disappears, everything in Al-Sayegh's life, was fettered to the trench and the camp. The battlefield became narrower and narrower. In "The Last Stations...The Beginning Of Madness", he announces:

Here I am, looking through a window's slot
To the street
Which become
Narrower...
Narrower...
Narrower... [427 L67-71]

Commenting on this state of actual and metaphorical narrowness, Al-Sayegh explains, "In reading this poem, one finds a self not a subject matter, a sensitive feeling not a superficial outward description, a deep personal wound not a military epic. Here, everything in the poet's life becomes one thing: a hole."[14]

Being psychologically destroyed as a result of the protracted war, the poet wants something that helps him to forget his painful and traumatic war experiences. He longs for the country he wishes it to be. He metaphorically compares it to a woman with whom he falls passionately in love. Like his country, he cannot forget her nor replace her with another woman. But the poet is fully aware that there is no escape from the terrible situation he finds himself in, however vast the earth is. In the form of command, he addresses himself

Or...
Run for it

Right now...
   From such impossible death
(-for there's no way out...
The earth is narrower than we thought
...narrower than that miser's palm... ['A Sky In A Helmet'
431. L23-29]

In spite of this portentous atmosphere, the poet decides to challenge this 'impossible death'. However, he is given a terrible shock upon realizing that he has only one helmet and that he has to choose to use it, in the protection of either his country or his head, both of which are already pierced:

I fell...
and my homeland gathered me in...
And we raced to the barricade
Challenging death together
Which of us will protect -
O my homeland-
         his own head...?
We have just one helmet...
         just one. [A Sky In A Helmet'432- 435. L 63-68]

The act of defiance implies some sense of hope and positive expectation. In spite of the large number of holes which nourish the rivers of death with the soldiers' blood in Al-Sayegh's sky, self, life, and anthology. He is able to turn them, metaphorically speaking, into small windows through which he looks forward to more promising and beautiful things, like hopes and life's desires.

In "A Preliminary Prologue", Al-Sayegh puts the helmet to another use. The fall of the helmets stand for the fall of his friends/ comrades-in-arms one by one. He consciously lets the helmet of his 'postponed' death fall to allow himself to sleep soundly, dream and hope:

A helmet fell down...
Then another...
Then another...
Then another...
I looked at my postponed death..
Coldly staring at me
It put off it's helmet..
And slept ['First Inaugurated' 423 L15-22]

Here the poet wonders about the reason that makes the war unable, unlike death, to put off it's helmet and sleep quietly.

With the act of 'falling down' which stands for death and the natural or inevitable companionship of soldiers in the battle fields. Al-Sayegh was able to create a kind of an outlet, though poetic, to give a full psychological vent to his feelings of frustration and disappointment. In a series of impassioned images, he talks about the postponement of death which gives him some hope. By personifying death, i.e., treating it as if it was a soldier who could also let his helmet drop, Al-Sayegh gives the impression that even death will fall asleep and let the soldier, by mistake, survive.

In the opening lines of the same poem, the artillery is personified. The soldiers are busy preparing the abominable breakfast for the artillery, which stands for the continuation of war that demands more and more casualties. The use of adjectives such as 'abominable', 'loathsome', and 'detested', stands for Al-Sayegh's deep abhorrence and hatred of war. While the poet's country keeps counting its "splinters and martyrs" [L4], the poet himself tries to create an optimistic atmosphere to heal his psychological wounds. Therefore he adds, that just as he is eager to put an end to this war, so also do his friends/fellow soldiers want to put an end to the bombardment of the artillery:

.. *The poem does not consent to me.*

The homeland was

On the front rampart...

Busy in counting his splinters and martyrs.

And my friends are preparing

Some abominable breakfast

For the artillery,

And waiting to put an end..

For the banquet of war [423 L 1-9]

Al-Sayegh keeps on personifying the weapons of war, which are performing a number of human activities like 'passing by', 'counting', and 'failing to love' ['A Train' 467 L29,31,36]. Paradoxically, he accuses the artillery of insensitivity, of being unable to enumerate its victims. Being famous for mingling the vocabularies of love with the vocabularies of war, Al-Sayegh wonders if the artillery were good at falling in love. He bitterly wishes that it would stop killing the soldiers and instead busy itself with loving them.

In his poems, Al-Sayegh often questions the nature of war and its impact on people. He often questions the ability of love to thrive under the threatening bombs of war. He usually senses, the frightening presence of all accidental shots lurking somewhere in the frontlines, in wait for the next chance to end his life. In "Train", from his diwan *Birds Don't Love Bullets* (1986) he gives full vent to his inner fears:

In the last evening of shrapnel..,
          I shall gather up-Like the poems-
The years of my life span
I shall classify them…
May be, I shall- in a moment-
Write off half of them
May be, an accidental shot
Will strike off the other half [466 L 7-14]

Al-Sayegh, used to closely tie the number of his years to the number of his poems. He is afraid of losing the remaining years of his life by an accidental shot. Therefore, he is determined to protect them by writing poems and indirectly using their words as shields to protect him from the abyss of mortality. In "Train", he compares himself to a 'loaf of bread'. He says:

Like a loaf of bread…
The shrapnel are divided into the
Cells of my blood.
I shall sit on the bench in a station,
Waiting for
A shot!
Night watchmen
Or women ['Train' 467-468 L 41-48]

The choice of the sources of threat and oppression is significant here. As 'a shot' is a symbol of war and death; 'night watchman' is a symbol of intellectual terror and close surveillance; whilst women are a symbol of normal peace time and family life which the poet is deprived of. In fact, feelings of panic and dismay took hold of the poet since the moment he arrived at the battle field. He is afraid of killing someone else or else be killed. He is alarmed by the prospects of losing his darlings and friends, of having a physical disability or experiencing other types of disruptive and paralysing events.

This tendency on the part of Al-Sayegh, to deal with what is familiar and customary in the soldiers' daily life, in order to spotlight the tragic and heart-rending; is what distinguishes the poet and makes him a "real poet who has the ability to prove that the everyday poem is worthy of life, love, and admiration".[15]

This draws our attention to "Ticket Girl" which tells of another relatively mundane occurrence. The girl of the poem deals, as part of her job, with different sorts of hands that are *"dusty, usurious, indifferent... pugnacious... and rough"*. [436 L11-14] The window that separate her from the theatre or cinema goers is again a small window that towers over the wider world; but the girl can see nothing of this world except what the window allows her: the "fingers and the palm of the hands". The fingers and the palms are as important to the ticket girl as for the soldiers who use them to hold the guns that protect their lives. They are always afraid of losing some of their fingers, a hand, a leg, or all of them. Here the chopped fingers are a symbol of everything that war represents, of its pitilessness and inhumanity. The soldier whose three fingers had been chopped in an offensive against the enemy lines, is afraid of the ticket girl's reaction when stretching his hand to get the ticket:

... He will walk to the booth
Perturbed, at a loss,
He thinks "she may gasp in astonishment
for seeing my chopped fingers,
my severed branches"
The shells may teach her
That fingers -in the war-
.... Are just like tickets. [437 L33-40]

As Al-Masri points out, the whole anthology is a "testimony to Al-Sayegh's tendency to deal with the ordinary and mundane as a pivotal cause and concern; to link the ordinary occurrences and make them a sign of general, moral important ones. He may go further as to aggrandize the ordinary, making it equal in importance or perhaps more important than the general".[16]

In this anthology, Al-Sayegh often talks about the streets, buses, friends, women, newspapers, telephones, branches, cities and about the war as a daily event that people become accustomed to during the long years of fighting. Like the resources of his country that were geared to war time needs, these people, places and items are geared to emphasize the ugliness and unsightliness of war. In "The Last Stations…The Beginning Of Madness", he is determined to tell his anonymous beloved about

..... the spittle of
The city
About the daily newspapers, and
The war,
About the lonely benches like me... [428 L 110-114]

Reading carefully Al-Sayegh's anthologies, one gets the impression that he is always "wholly engaged in shedding light on the dark hidden corners whether they are related to one's feeling or the daily rhythms of one's life".[17] In this sense, Al-Sayegh's poems cannot be read unless taking into consideration, the general context in which they are being written. For is the war, which continues to haunt his life and writings even after its end and his transfer away from the battle fields.

In *A Cloud Of Glue* (1993), which he wrote after the end of the war, the war atrocities and repercussions loomed large in the poems. In truth, Al-Sayegh still sensed the painful presence of war, long after the end of the military operations and his discharge from the army. The bitter and shocking memories of war kept haunting him, deeply affecting the nature of his longing for his beloveds and friends. It also affected his relationship with Nature itself. As Kareem Sha'alan points out, the vocabularies of war "forcibly imposed themselves on the poet's life and poetry. Whether consciously or unconsciously, Al-Sayegh cannot escape them".[18]

To sum up, Al-Sayegh's poetry is a mirror that reflects the multilayered psychological conditions, under which he was living in each stage of his life. This makes his poetry as diverse as life itself. Therefore the most noticeable feature of this poetry is the overwhelming presence of war as a theme and metaphor. War and it's ramifications are so significant, they surpass all other themes. Al-Sayegh uses vocabularies of war even in his courtship of his sweetheart. In this sense, he was able to write "love poems in terms of war".[19]

NOTES

1- Ghalib Al- Shabinder, "Qera'a Jawanea Fi Dewan Adnan Al-Sayegh 'Sama'a Fi Khutha'" (An In-depth Reading of Adnan Al-Sayegh's Diwan 'Sky In A Helmet'), Al- Nahdha Newspaper, Sweden, 153, May, 17, 2004.

2- Hatim Al- Sagar, "Aldakhil Althaiq.. And Alkharig Almutase" (The Narrow Inside.. And Spacious Outside), Al-Joumhouria Newspaper, Baghdad, 1988.

3- Adnan Al-Sayegh, Al- A'amal Al- Sha'aria (Poetic Works), (Beirut: AIRP, 2004) 404

4- Ibid. 694

5- Hassan Al- Sudani, "Adnan Al-Sayegh: seera Qalamea" (Biography)
    http://www.adnanalsayegh.com/ara/index.asp accessed at July, 28, 2003.

6- All subsequent poems are from: Adnan Al-Sayegh, Al-A'amal Al-Sha'aria, unless otherwise indicated.

7- Tarad Al- Kubaisi, "Intathireni Taht Nasb Alhuria" (Wait For Me Under The Statue Of Liberty), Al- Thawra Newspaper, Baghdad: April, 18, 1985.

8- Adnan Al-Sayegh, Al- A'amal Al- Sha'aria (Poetic Works), 688

9- Qaes Kadhem Al-Janabi, "Thuqub Fi Khutha.. Samaa Fi Khutha: Alyaumi Wal Ma'loof Fi Qasedat Alharb" (Hole In A Helmet.. Sky In A Helmet: The Daily And The Familiar In The War Poem), Al- qadsia Newspaper, Sept., 14, 1990.

10- Khalid Mohammed Al- Masri, "Alharb Fi Alqaseda Alyawmia Wal qaseda Alyawmia Fil harb: Qera'a Fi Dewan 'Samaa Fi Khutha' Li Adnan Al-Sayegh" (War In The Daily Poem And Daily Poem In The War: Reading In Adnan Al-Sayegh's Anthology 'Sky In A Helmet"), Al- Thefaf Magazine, Austria:9 , Feb., 2002.

11- Ghalib Al- Shabinder, "Qera'a Jawanea Fi Dewan Adnan Al-Sayegh".

12- Ibid.

13- Ibid.

14- Hatim Al- Sagar, "Aldakhil Althaiq .. And Alkharig Almutase".

15- Abed Al-Jabar Dawood Al- Basri, "Qera'a Fi Dewan Adnan Al-Sayegh: Qasa'id Al-Harb" (Reading In Adnan Al-Sayegh's Anthology: War Poems), Al- Joumhouria Newspaper, 1985.

16- Khalid Mohammed Al- Masri, "Alharb Fi Alqaseda Alyawmia".

17- Abd Al- Rahman Al- Rubae'i, "Adnan Al-Sayegh Sha'er Kharajah Min Alharb Sudfah" (Adnan Al-Sayegh A Poet Who survived the *war accidentally), Al- Qudus Al- Arabi Newspaper, London: 2095, Feb., 2, 1996.*

18- *Kareem Sha'alan, "Ra'ehat Alharb Fi Ghaimat Alsamgh" (The Smell Of War In 'A cloud of glue'), Al- Wefaq Newspaper, London: 299, Jan. 15, 1998.*

19- *Hamza Mustafa, "Mushkelat Alta'sees Fi Qasedat Alharb" (The Problems Of Foundations In War Poem), Al- Aqlaam Magazine, Nov. 12, 1987.*

BIBILIOGRAPHY

Al- Basri, Abed Al- Jabar Dawood. "Qera'a Fi Dewan Adnan Al-Sayegh: Qasa'id Al- Harb" (Reading In Adnan Al- Sayegh's Diwan: War Poems). Al- Joumhouria Newspaper. 1985.

Al- Janabi, Qaes Kadhem. "Thuqub Fi Khutha.. Samaa Fi Khutha: Alyaumi Wal Ma'loof Fi Qasedat Alharb" (Hole In A Helmet.. Sky In A Helmet: The Daily And The Familiar In The War Poem). Al- Qadsia Newspaper. Sept., 14, 1990.

Al- Kubaisi, Tarad. "Intathireni Taht Nasb Alhuria" (Wait For Me Under The Statue Of Liberty). Al- Thawra Newspaper. Baghdad: April, 18, 1985.

Al- Masri, Khalid Mohammed. "Alharb Fi Alqaseda Alyawmia Wal qaseda Alyawmia Fil Harb: Qera'a Fi Dewan 'Samaa Fi Khutha' Li Adnan Al-Sayegh" (War In The Daily Poem And Daily Poem In The War: Reading In Adnan Al- Sayegh's Anthology 'Sky In A Helmet'"). Al- Thefaf Magazine. Austria: 9. Feb. 2002

Al- Rubae'i, Abd Al- Rahman. "Adnan Al-Sayegh Sha'er Kharajah Min Alharb Sudfah" (Adnan Al-Sayegh A Poet Who Survived The War Accidentally). Al- Qudus Al- Arabi Newspaper. London 6.

Al-Sayegh, Adnan. Al- A'amal Al- Sha'aria (Poetic Works). Beirut: AIRP, 2004.

Al- Shabinder, Ghalib. "Qera'a Jawanea Fi Dewan Adnan Al-Sayegh 'Sama'a Fi Khutha'" (An In-depth Reading of Adnan Al-Sayegh's Divan 'Sky In A Helmet'). Al-Nahdha Newspaper. Sweden, 153. May, 17, 2004.

Al- Sudani, Hassan. "Adnan Al-Sayegh: seera Qalamea" (Biography) http://www.adnanalsayegh.com/ara/index.asp accessed at July, 28, 2013.

Mustafa, Hamza. "Mushkelat Alta'sees Fi Qasedat Alharb" (The Problems Of Foundations In War Poem). Al- Aqlam Magazine. Nov. 12, 1987.

Sha'alan, Kareem. "Ra'ehat Alharb Fi Ghaimat Alsamgh"(The Smell Of War In 'A cloud of glue'). Al-Wefaq Newspaper. London: 299. Jan. 15, 1998.

A Technical Study of the Poetry of Adnan Al-Sayegh

Abstract from the thesis "The Poetry of Adnan Al-Sayegh, a Technical Study". Submitted by Arif Al-Saadi for his Master of Arts, degree. It was awarded a 'distinction' by the Department of Arabic Language/ College of Education / University of Al-Mustansiriyah/ Baghdad, 2006 AD.

Translated by Ali Al- Manna
Edited by Marga Burgui-Artajo

Adnan al-Sayegh is a poet who, burned by the fires of love and war, has emerged from them soothed by their rain, transforming his calm and stillness into clouds that wetted the ashes of an ugly war whose face he wanted to expose. He has tried to sow seeds of life within the trenches and front lines. This is the poet's life:

He brings much of his experience to his everyday poems, often being able to elevate the marginal, and forgotten aspects of life to a brilliant poetic level, invulnerable to the rust of life. Al-Sayegh is a poet who has accomplished much in terms of both quality and quantity; he is at his pinnacle as a poet, which is the reason why I chose to study his work.

He belongs to the generation of Iraqi poets known as the Eighties Movement, who lived during the Iraqi-Iranian war. The topic of war is thus inherent in their poetry. Al-Sayegh has lived a tough life. A life full of wardens, guards and killers. However in contrast to the difficulties that he has lived through, he is an optimistic lover of life. This is the reason why the interaction between his work and his hard life, has given birth to some warm romantic poetry.

In the later period of his life he was forced into exile, to live in a snowy country where everything was available and beautiful. A country where he could experience living a life of freedom and reassurance, far away from the sunny yet sinister Iraq. As he lived through this new existence, he wondered if it would affect his writing? How will it react to this new environment, where freedom has replaced oppression? Al-Sayegh's poems at this stage appear to reflect his new living circumstances.

His poetic lexicon still full of guardians, policemen and fences, is starting to take a different turn: words like 'soot', 'passing wind' and paunches, are found in his recent poems. With regard to this, the poet says: 'It has altered my writing style. I now encompass freedom of expression, dreams, memories, imagination etc. However no sooner do I pick up my pen to start writing about the massive forests, covered in snow, then nightmares of war and graves haunt me and take away all the beauty and spirituality from my lines.' He adds: 'How can I get rid of dirt, wires and wars with nice dreams and a straightforward pen?' He comments 'In the past I had to resort to the technique of camouflaged language and that was a stimulus towards adventure, challenge and creativity...' With regard to the change of language in his poems published outside Iraq...He adds 'It reflects the release of my memory, a memory overflowing with blood scenes and saturated with the smell of black sorrow'.

Al-Sayegh always brings women and nature together. His love poems written in Iraq rarely lack a link between the eyes of his beloved and nature. Some critics attribute this link to a romantic tendency frequent in young poets. Reading through Al-Sayegh's poetry, I could not separate the words he uses for women from those that he uses for nature – they are mixed, syntactically and semantically. I have studied both the vocabulary of love and the vocabulary of nature, searching for his ability to divert the denotative meaning of a word or phrase into its poetic shadow. He uses lexical terms such as 'rainy eyes', 'clamorous eyes', 'green eyes', 'morning eyes', 'rain is clouded in your eyes', 'my heart port', 'my heart butterfly', 'my heart branch', 'my heart leaves', 'my heart gardens', 'my heart nursery' and 'my heart bud'.

But a more extensive vocabulary forms part of his poetic

language, with words such as: 'mornings', 'dawn', 'spirit', 'trees', 'wind', 'flower', 'window', 'dream', and 'female' Going through his poetic language in his love and nature poems, the researcher found that the word 'heart' is ubiquitous, being often accompanied by the phrase 'grass-covered'. You will rarely find a poem without one of these two words, which leads Al-Sayegh to a certain reiteration; his heart is always connected with 'farm', 'grass', 'leaves',' buds', 'nursery', 'butterflies', 'windows', etc. He writes,

It is the wakeful homeland
On the firebrand of connection
Extending from the bottom of your eyes
To the ports of my heart:
Delicious, pretty and lightening,
like all mornings ... When I see you
Parading in your dress embroidered with daisies
A flower of affection,
The butterflies of my heart become cheerful
And I go on.

This stanza is from the first poem written by Al-Sayegh, called 'Flirtation. It was published in his book 'Wait for me under the Statue of Liberty'. It lacks the usual detailed description of his beloved that we find in other poems. This is a poem consisting of two themes: his beloved and nature in its various forms. Important elements of the poem are as follows: 'the bottom of your eyes', 'butterflies of my heart', 'ports of my heart', 'sparrows of our village', 'windows of my heart'. Its vocabulary includes 'mornings', 'daisy', 'flower', 'affection', 'poem', and 'gardens'.

In some poems it seems that Al-Sayegh focuses his attention on a location. He is from a town called al- Kufa complete with its farms, palms, rivers and gardens., As soon as he leaves this sylvan environment, he recreates it in poetic form. In so doing he moves from the stillness of nature to movement and growth, as he personifies sparrows and gardens to talk about his beloved.

As for his heart, that small organ from which feelings of love

91

and warmth are said to flow, he uses it to perform different roles. He links it to a port or harbour and accordingly connects it with the sea. He links it also with butterflies, with various connote meanings such as a garden or farm. At the end of the poem he returns to the heart and endows it with windows 'I open all windows of my heart.. to you.. I whisper in your ears... come in safely' Words like heart, ears, sparrows and gardens' have a linguistic function other than the one we are used to. In his poem 'In the waiting for the poem' he says;

I become confused on how the poem is created!
And it lashes the shores of my heart like a wave
...

And from where does the poem come?
What is It's title?
I ask all the roads:
Did my frivolous... lady pass by?
I ask all friends:
Who has seen my sweetheart with a shirt embroidered with a
dream of stars?
Running
In my hear farms...

The poem seems to deal with a woman chased by the poet, she quarrels with him and becomes obstinate. The poet personifies the poem as a female – it has white laces and a drowsy look. A romantic perfume pervades many of his poems. However, the warm and soft words in his poems do not always reflect a romantic attitude. This is what we can conclude from this particular poem, which is full of words such as 'remote banks' 'my sweetheart', 'starlets', 'fragrance', 'white laces', 'drowsy look', 'transparent glasses', and 'rustling of branches'.

As for his war poems, they have nothing in common with the poems of Enthusiasm, well known in the Arab tradition. The poems of Enthusiasm are confined to one point of view and one purpose. In them we find enthusiasm and pride, as well as a detailed description of the feats of the poet, his tribe, leader, army and horses. However they never speak of weaknesses and strengths, nor do they give voice to other opinions as Al-Sayegh does in his poems. He looks at the war in a different way. His poetic role is not to document events and glories, but rather to reach and relate the core of the situation. In his poetic lexicon we find words such as, 'soldiers', 'veiling', 'bullet', 'martyr', 'trenches', 'bombardment', 'borders', 'widow', 'missile', 'barracks', 'pavement of stations', 'battlefields', 'mine', 'guns,' and 'lieutenant…' When somebody reads Al-Sayegh's poems, they will remember the stories in the early eighties of soldiers, returning home during their monthly leave. For their stories are about camps, life in the trenches and their own personal worries.

Al-Sayegh succeeds in technically exploiting the term 'war' with all the ugliness and death that it carries, by creating a new and wider artistic picture of the period. It is as if he has opened a window to allow the light to traverse the dark wall. All his poems about war and love, plus a third group of poems that also focus on the daily neglected marginal issues, were all written in Iraq.

The poetry that Al-Sayegh wrote outside Iraq deals with exile and it is substantially different from the poetry written in Iraq. His poetic imagery starts to take a minor role and does not constitute a basic element of the structure of the exile poems. His language now focuses on indication rather than image.

It is difficult to arrange Al-Sayegh's poetry into various genres as it is not possible to separate war from nature or love in his poems. The researcher concludes that Al-Sayegh's war poems could be called 'romantic war poems' that condemn war:

I proclaim: Tomorrow
I will stretch out over the broad day
I will search among the bombs and the mud
For what is left of my life and my friends
I will fill my lungs with alleys and jasmine,
And will return home without manifestos
Carving my dreams into corpses and outrages.
Terms relating to war such as 'planes' bombs, corpses,
outrages and manifesto are juxtaposed with terms relating to
life such as 'broad day,' 'friends,' 'jasmine' 'my dream' and

'clouds.' The war appears as a monster facing the poet, who armed with words of beauty tries to minimize it's ugliness.

In his poems, words denoting death and life coexist alongside those denoting beauty and ugliness.

I will stretch out over the broad day,	life
Shaded by clouds instead of planes,	life
I will search among the bombs and the mud	death
For what is left of my life and my friends.	life
I will fill my lungs with alleys and jasmine	life
And return home without manifestos	life
Carving my dreams into corpses and outrages.	death

Al-Sayegh's poems of the battlefield reflect a dichotomy. Hardly has a 'death' word or sentence appeared before he creates an antithetical term or sentence to lighten that darkness and tension.

Having shed some light on the poetic dictionary of Al-Sayegh's works published inside Iraq, I can now deal with his collections published outside the country. Anybody familiar with Al-Sayegh's lexical terms will find them now totally different – new terms like 'alienation', 'homesickness', 'exile', 'prisons', 'freedom', etc.' are found in his poetry of exile.

After leaving Iraq, Al-Sayegh traversed through a number of Arab countries and lived in some of their cities until he finally settled in Sweden. During this time he created many poetic works and for every capital in which he resided, he has a poetic memory. These travels yielded terms relating to homesickness and alienation. Al-Sayegh says:

I have a homeland in the shadow of palm-trees fenced with rifles
Oh! How can I reach it?
And the distance has become so wide between us and the gentle reproof
How can I see close friends

Who were made absent in dungeons?
Or who put weight on the scales
Or who were handed to the dust?
It is an ordeal to find – after twenty years –
The bridge is not the one you crossed once
And the skies are not the same skies
And people are haunted with absence.

In this poem, entitled 'doors', we find a different expression of alienation that implies his deep philosophical thoughts:

I knock on a door
I open it
But I see nothing except myself as a door
I open it
And I enter
But there is nothing except another door
Oh! Lord
How many doors separate me from myself?

In this poem there are no explicit words referring to homesickness or exile, however it does in an implicit way suggest exile and alienation. "Door and myself " are the key word, to which all the verbs and pronouns are related. Alienation and freedom are suggested in this poem by the opening of 'doors'. However whilst "myself" may physically "open" a "door" emotionally he is unable to do so. This is made apparent by the rhetorical question "Oh Lord" How many doors separate me from myself?" The poet has chosen to use a simple noun such as "door" to express his philosophical attitude to life.